Mary Washington

Kitchen Chronicles: Tales and Recipes from the Heart of Cooking

Introduction

In the clamoring heart of culinary investigation, where the ringing of utensils and the sizzling of dish make an ensemble, we find Cook Isabella, a culinary maestro enthusiastically that rises above the bounds of a customary kitchen. "Kitchen Narratives: Stories and Recipes from the Core of Cooking" welcomes you to set out on a gastronomic odyssey that goes past the simple planning of dinners.

Mary Washington

Chapter 1

The Aroma of Memories

The book opens with Chef Isabella's childhood, where the kitchen served as a hub for family gatherings and shared meals. The scents of spices and the sizzle of pans became the backdrop for the creation of lifelong memories. Each recipe, a chapter in her life story, carries the aroma of cherished moments.

Chapter 2

Culinary Heritage Unveiled

As Chef Isabella ventures into her culinary roots, readers are taken on a global journey. Tales of ancestral kitchens, handed-down recipes, and the rich tapestry of diverse culinary traditions unfold. Each dish becomes a vessel for preserving cultural heritage, a link to the past that is as relevant today as it was generations ago.

Chapter 3

The Dance of Ingredients

Chef Isabella introduces readers to the rhythmic dance of ingredients. Through vivid descriptions and anecdotes, she unveils the magic that occurs when seemingly ordinary components come together to create extraordinary flavors. The kitchen becomes a stage, and each recipe is a choreographed performance.

Chapter 4

Lessons from the Flame

Amidst the flickering flames of the stove, Chef Isabella shares the lessons she learned from the heat of the kitchen. From resilience to patience, cooking becomes a metaphor for life's challenges. Through failures and triumphs, she imparts wisdom gained from years of mastering the culinary craft.

Chapter 5

Culinary Crossroads

The narrative takes a turn as Chef Isabella recounts her encounters with diverse cuisines. Traveling to far-off lands, she discovers the universal language of food. Each encounter broadens her culinary palette, leading to the creation of unique, fusion recipes that marry the best of global flavors.

Chapter 6

The Heartfelt Table

At the heart of Chef Isabella's journey is the communal aspect of dining. The dining table becomes a sacred space where relationships are nourished, and conversations flow freely. Recipes are shared not just for their flavors but for the stories they carry, fostering a sense of connection among those who gather.

Chapter 7

Seasons on the Plate

With a poetic touch, Chef Isabella explores the seasonal ebb and flow of ingredients. She celebrates the beauty of adapting to nature's bounty, creating dishes that resonate with the colors and moods of each season. The kitchen becomes a canvas, and the recipes are strokes of culinary art.

Chapter 8

Beyond the Recipe Card

As the book concludes, Chef Isabella reflects on the profound impact of the kitchen on her life. Beyond the tangible recipes, she emphasizes the intangible elements – the joy of creating, the healing power of comfort food, and the love infused into every dish. "Kitchen Chronicles" is not just a cookbook; it's a testament to the soulful journey of cooking from the heart.

Chapter 9

Culinary Resilience

Chef Isabella delves into the challenges faced in the culinary world. From kitchen mishaps to unexpected ingredient shortages, she shares stories of resilience. Each setback becomes an opportunity for innovation, and readers gain insight into the tenacity required to navigate the unpredictable terrain of a professional kitchen.

Chapter 10

The Artistry of Presentation

Moving beyond the flavors, Chef Isabella reveals the artistry behind plating. With anecdotes of culinary competitions and high-stakes events, she demonstrates how the presentation of a dish is a form of edible art. The kitchen becomes a studio, and each plate is a masterpiece, reflecting the chef's creativity and attention to detail.

Chapter 11

Culinary Conversations

Chef Isabella explores the conversations that unfold in the kitchen. From passionate debates over the perfect recipe to the silent understanding between chefs working in tandem, the kitchen becomes a space for dialogue. Through shared experiences, the camaraderie among those who appreciate the art of cooking is celebrated.

Mary Washington

Chapter 12

The Evolution of Taste

As Chef Isabella's culinary journey progresses, she reflects on the evolving nature of taste. Palates change, culinary trends come and go, and she adapts her recipes to reflect the dynamic landscape of food preferences. The kitchen becomes a laboratory, and each experiment contributes to the ever-evolving tapestry of flavors.

Chapter 13

Culinary Legacy

In a poignant chapter, Chef Isabella contemplates the idea of leaving behind a culinary legacy. She shares her hopes of inspiring future generations of chefs and home cooks. Each recipe becomes a legacy marker, a testament to a life dedicated to the pursuit of gastronomic excellence.

Chapter 14

The Joy of Teaching

Chef Isabella's narrative takes a turn as she discusses her experiences as a culinary educator. The kitchen transforms into a classroom, and recipes become lessons in technique and creativity. Through teaching, she discovers the profound satisfaction of passing on the torch and witnessing the culinary journeys of her students.

Chapter 15

Culinary Adventures in Unlikely Places

The book concludes with Chef Isabella's tales of culinary exploration in unexpected locations. From impromptu roadside stalls to humble family kitchens, she discovers that remarkable dishes can emerge from the most unassuming places. The kitchen, in its varied forms, becomes a universal space for culinary discovery.

Chapter 16

Culinary Traditions Reimagined

As Chef Isabella continues her journey, she explores the concept of reimagining culinary traditions. Drawing inspiration from classic recipes passed down through generations, she infuses modern twists, breathing new life into time-honored dishes. The kitchen becomes a crossroads of tradition and innovation, where heritage is honored while

Mary Washington

embracing the excitement of
culinary experimentation.

Chapter 17

The Healing Potency of Food

In a deeply personal chapter, Chef Isabella shares stories of how food becomes a source of comfort and healing. From crafting nourishing soups during challenging times to preparing meals that speak the language of love, she reveals the transformative power of food beyond its taste. The kitchen evolves into a sanctuary, offering solace and restoration through carefully curated recipes.

Mary Washington

Chapter 18

Culinary Rituals

Chef Isabella explores the idea of culinary rituals, where the act of cooking transcends mere sustenance. From Sunday family dinners to elaborate holiday feasts, she illustrates how these rituals create bonds and memories. The kitchen becomes a sacred space where routines and traditions intertwine, shaping the fabric of familial and communal connections.

Chapter 19

The Global Pantry

Venturing into the heart of culinary diversity, Chef Isabella introduces readers to the concept of a global pantry. Drawing from ingredients spanning continents, she showcases the beauty of creating harmonious fusions. The kitchen transforms into a treasure trove of international flavors, demonstrating that borders dissolve when it comes to the universality of good food.

Mary Washington

Chapter 20

Culinary Reflections

In a reflective chapter, Chef Isabella contemplates the ever-changing landscape of the culinary world. From trends that come and go to the enduring classics, she shares insights into the cyclical nature of food culture. The kitchen becomes a mirror reflecting societal shifts, reminding us that the art of cooking is both timeless and constantly evolving.

Chapter 21

The Culinary Explorer's Toolkit

Chef Isabella opens her toolkit, revealing the essential ingredients, techniques, and philosophies that define her culinary approach. From the precision of knife skills to the intuition behind flavor pairings, she imparts the wisdom accumulated over years of exploration. The kitchen transforms into an alchemical workshop, where a dash of creativity and a pinch of

Mary Washington

expertise create culinary
wonders.

Chapter 22

Culinary Harmony

In the penultimate chapter, Chef Isabella delves into the concept of culinary harmony. Exploring the interplay of textures, flavors, and aromas, she guides readers through the art of achieving balance in every dish. The kitchen becomes a symphony, and each recipe is a carefully orchestrated composition aimed at creating a harmonious culinary experience.

Chapter 23

Culinary Collaboration

In this chapter, Chef Isabella explores the power of collaboration in the kitchen. She shares stories of working alongside fellow chefs, artists, and culinary enthusiasts. From pop-up events to collaborative cookbooks, the kitchen becomes a space for synergy, where diverse talents converge to create culinary masterpieces that transcend individual creativity.

Mary Washington

Chapter 24

The Essence of Seasonal Eating

Chef Isabella delves into the significance of seasonal eating, emphasizing the connection between food and nature's cycles. She discusses the joy of anticipating and savoring ingredients at their peak, celebrating the ephemerality of flavors. The kitchen transforms into a seasonal tableau, where each recipe reflects the bounty of the earth during its designated time.

Mary Washington

Chapter 25

Culinary Innovations

As a forward-thinking chef, Chef Isabella shares tales of culinary innovations that have shaped her approach. From molecular gastronomy experiments to exploring plant-based alternatives, she embraces the ever-expanding boundaries of culinary creativity. The kitchen becomes a laboratory, and each experiment contributes to the continuous evolution of her culinary repertoire.

Mary Washington

Chapter 26

Culinary Trademarks

In this chapter, Chef Isabella reflects on the development of her own culinary trademarks. Whether it's a signature spice blend, a unique plating technique, or a secret ingredient, she discusses the importance of personal touches that define a chef's style. The kitchen becomes a canvas for self-expression, where each dish carries the unmistakable imprint of its creator.

Mary Washington

Chapter 27

The Culinary Pilgrimage

Embarking on a culinary pilgrimage, Chef Isabella recounts her travels to iconic food destinations. From bustling markets in Marrakech to Michelin-starred restaurants in Tokyo, she shares the transformative experiences that have enriched her culinary perspective. The kitchen becomes a passport to global flavors, and each journey leaves an indelible mark on her culinary narrative.

Mary Washington

Chapter 28

Culinary Wisdom from Elders

Chef Isabella pays homage to the invaluable wisdom passed down by culinary elders. Through heartwarming anecdotes, she highlights the role of mentors and seasoned chefs who have shaped her culinary philosophy. The kitchen becomes a continuum of knowledge, with each recipe carrying the collective wisdom of those who came before.

Chapter 29

Culinary Rejuvenation

In this chapter, Chef Isabella explores the concept of culinary rejuvenation. She shares stories of rediscovering forgotten recipes, reviving culinary traditions, and finding inspiration in unexpected places. The kitchen becomes a realm of rediscovery, where the past intertwines with the present to create a vibrant and rejuvenated culinary narrative.

Chapter 30

The Infinite Possibilities of the Culinary Canvas

As "Kitchen Chronicles" approaches its conclusion, Chef Isabella marvels at the infinite possibilities that lie within the culinary canvas. She encourages readers to view the kitchen as an ever-expanding realm of creativity, where there are no limits to what can be achieved. The book becomes an invitation for aspiring chefs and home cooks to embrace the boundless

Mary Washington

potential that awaits them in
their culinary journeys.

www.ingramcontent.com/pod-product-compliance
Lightning Source LLC
Chambersburg PA
CBHW070225260726
48658CB00006BA/2169